GOD MADE ME PERFECT!

Amayah's Amazing Birthmark

Written by: Candace McLaughlin
Illustrated by: Tekla Todria

ISBN: 9780578705422

This book is dedicated to my precious daughter Amayah. Thank you for your inspiration.

"Wake up, Amayah, its time to go to school!" Mom yelled into my room. I pulled the covers over my head.

"Aaah, Mama, just 5 more minutes, please!" I yelled back.

"I gave you 5 minutes, 10 minutes ago! Now its time to get up and do your morning routine! We are leaving for school in 30 minutes!"

Every morning I wake up, brush my teeth, wash my face, eat breakfast, and put on my makeup. That's the hardest part, the makeup. It usually takes me about 10 minutes to get it right! Now, why does a 10 year older have to wear makeup? I'm glad you asked.

I was born with a port wine stain on my face. It doesn't hurt. It's just a really red birthmark on my cheek. Sometimes, people stare at it. I was picked on a lot in first grade. Other children would laugh and make fun of me. It was really bad and for a long time, it was one of the main reasons why I never wanted to go to school.

Things are better when I hide it. When I put on makeup, I feel like a normal kid. My classmates will actually talk to me, sit with me at lunchtime, and no one calls me names anymore! It's much better this way!

"Class, we have a new student here today. Come on in, don't be shy," Mrs. Boston said. All of the students were waiting for the new kid to enter the classroom.

In came a happy little boy, smiling and laughing. He eagerly walked to the front and screamed at the top of his lungs, "Hi, everyone, my name is Eddy!"

"Kids, say hello back!" the teacher said. The whole classroom was amazed, in shock, and everyone stared at him. I was especially surprised and couldn't believe my eyes.

"Hey, new kid! What's that on your face?" Jeremy yelled across the room. Half of the class started laughing out loud and the other half was still staring in disbelief.

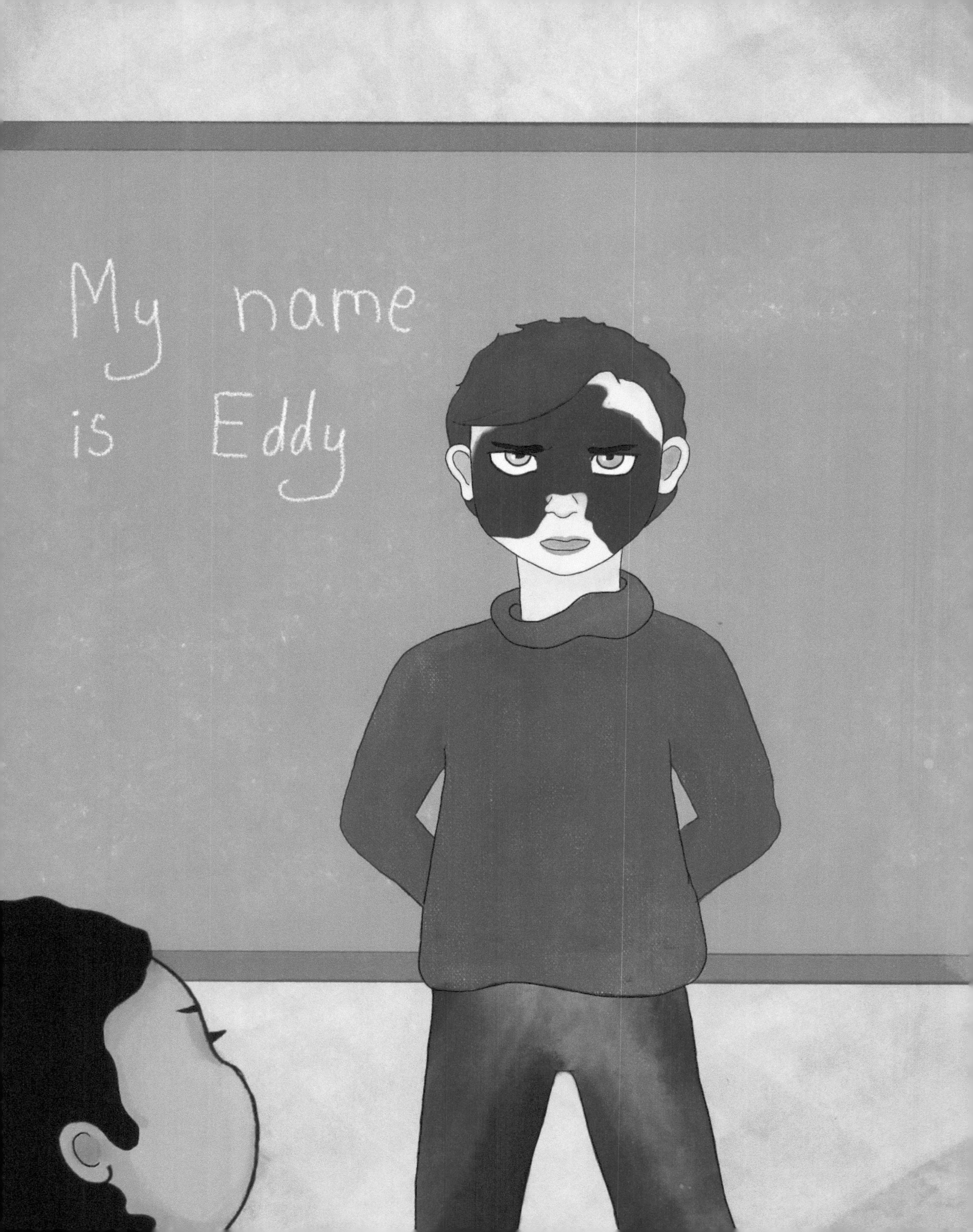
My name
is Eddy

"Well, I'm happy to tell you! Its my birthmark! Its called Melanocytic Nevus but I call it my super hero mask! God made me this way, because with Him, and my mask, I can face anything!" Eddy said while smirking. Eddy's birthmark was not like mine. His was dark and completely covered his eyes and forehead. He kind of looked like Batman which I thought was super awesome!

I couldn't believe what he said. I honestly started to feel scared for him because I knew the others were getting their insults and jokes prepared. However, after watching Eddy give his speech, it made me feel a little better about my own birthmark. I couldn't wait to talk to him about it.

Rrrrrriinnnnngggg…. The bell sounded, and it was lunch time! I used to dread going to lunch because that's usually when I would have the most problems out of my day. I really hope the new kid will be okay.

Eddy grabbed his lunch plate and looked for a table. He walked over to a lunch table with some of the other students from our class. Oh no Eddy, don't do it, please! They are going to get up and move! They are going to laugh at you! They are going to crack jokes! Oh I can't bare to watch this at all! I covered my eyes.

Then I heard laughing. I knew it! I just knew it! I have to do something. I can't let them bully Eddy like this. He's such a sweet kid! He doesn't deserve this type of treatment. I stood up and ran over to the table, ready to defend the new kid.

As soon as I stormed over and opened my mouth to give a smarty-pants remark, I saw Eddy laughing too and standing in a superhero stance. "What is he doing?" I thought to myself.

I walked over a little closer to get a good listen. I could hear Eddy going on and on. "Black Panther is so much cooler than Batman! You can't even compare the two!" Then, Jonathan pulled out a paper-made Batman mask that looked similar to Eddy's birthmark. I just knew this wasn't going to be good.

"I'm Batman!" Jonathan said in a dark and mysterious tone. Everyone started to laugh, even Eddy. I don't get it. The same classmates that picked on me for my birthmark since First Grade are now laughing and talking with Eddy about his.

Eddy stood up and began to put his plate away. I finally got enough courage to walk over and introduce myself. "Hi, I'm Amayah. Um… I'm in your class too."

"Hey Myah! What's going on?"

I went on to tell Eddy how courageous he was for standing up to Jeremy in class and how I could never be that brave.

"Oh, it was nothing. I used to get bullied a lot at my old school when I was younger. But I've learned that if you embrace it, love and accept yourself, others will learn to do the same thing," Eddy said with great confidence.

"I have a birthmark on my face too!" I blurted out. I quickly covered my mouth in embarrassment. I couldn't believe I said it that fast! Whew! I needed to get that out! It felt good to finally talk to someone about it other than my family.

"Well, where is it? I don't see anything," Eddy pondered. He began to inspect my face so hard that he could have stared a hole right through it!

"Oh, you see, I put makeup on over it every morning so the others won't make fun of me like they used to."

"Okay, go ahead! Let me see." Eddy took a napkin from his lunch plate and wet it with a little water. His hand started coming up towards my face.

"Nooo! What are you doing?" I shouted.

"Trust me," Eddy reassured. Eddy started wiping my face with the wet napkin until it revealed my rosy red birthmark that covered the side of my head down to my cheek and to my top lip.

"Aah ha! There we go. Perfect! You know, every superhero needs his sidekick," Eddy grabbed my hand and we walked over to the table where my classmates were still playing and eating.

"Ah hmm!" He cleared his throat loudly. "Attention everyone! I'm pleased to announce that I have found my new superhero sidekick! And if anyone has a problem with her, then they will have a problem with me!" Eddy laughed.

Everyone sitting at the table stopped what they were doing and began to stare at me. I could feel the heat from shame and the tears starting to form behind my eyes.

"Oh Amayah, you finally took off the makeup!" Brailey said. Brailey was the most popular girl in our class. Everyone loved her. I couldn't believe she remembered I had a birthmark. I was 6 years old when all of the bullying started—I figured they forgot about it. They hadn't mentioned it since.

Brailey stood up and walked over to me, examining my cheek. I took a step back. "Hmm, I never realized until now, your birthmark kind of looks like a red rose! Amayah, that's so cool… Amayah Rose! I love it, that's your new name!"

"WOW, that's actually not bad….I love it too!" I exclaimed. I felt great. The makeup was finally off and my courage was finally on! Then, something happened. One of my classmates brought over a drawing, a picture of me, with a rose on my cheek. At the bottom of the drawing it had my new name and a message: "Amayah Rose, You don't have to hide anymore because God made you perfect just the way you are!"

I hugged the drawing as tight as I could. "Thank you so much! I'll never lose it. I'm going to hang it up on my mirror as soon as I get home so every time I look at it, it'll remind me that I am confident, I am strong, and I am beautiful. And apparently, a superhero sidekick too!" We all laughed.

"Mom, I'm home!"

"Hey, Myah, how was your day?" Mom asked. I handed her the picture my classmate drew of me. She looked at me and said, "Um, Amayah, what happened to your makeup?" I told her all about Eddy and the eventful day I had.

"Mom, I don't need it any more! I'm perfect just the way I am, exactly how God made me!"

My mom smiled and grabbed me close. "Yes, baby, you are! I've always told you that." She kissed me on my rosy cheek. "Never forget it! You are amazing and you are beautiful! And you don't have to hide because God made you perfect just the way you are!"

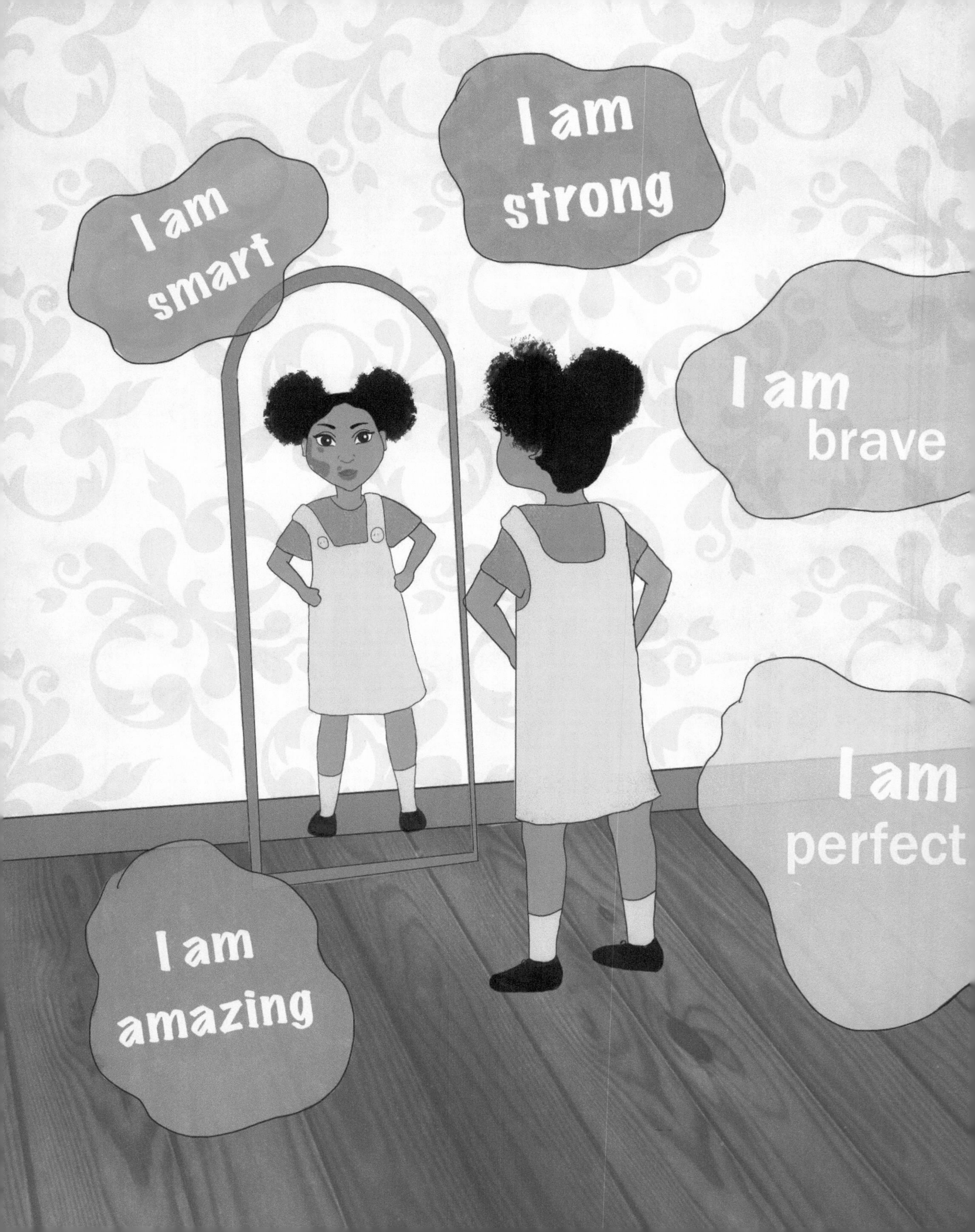
I am smart
I am strong
I am brave
I am perfect
I am amazing

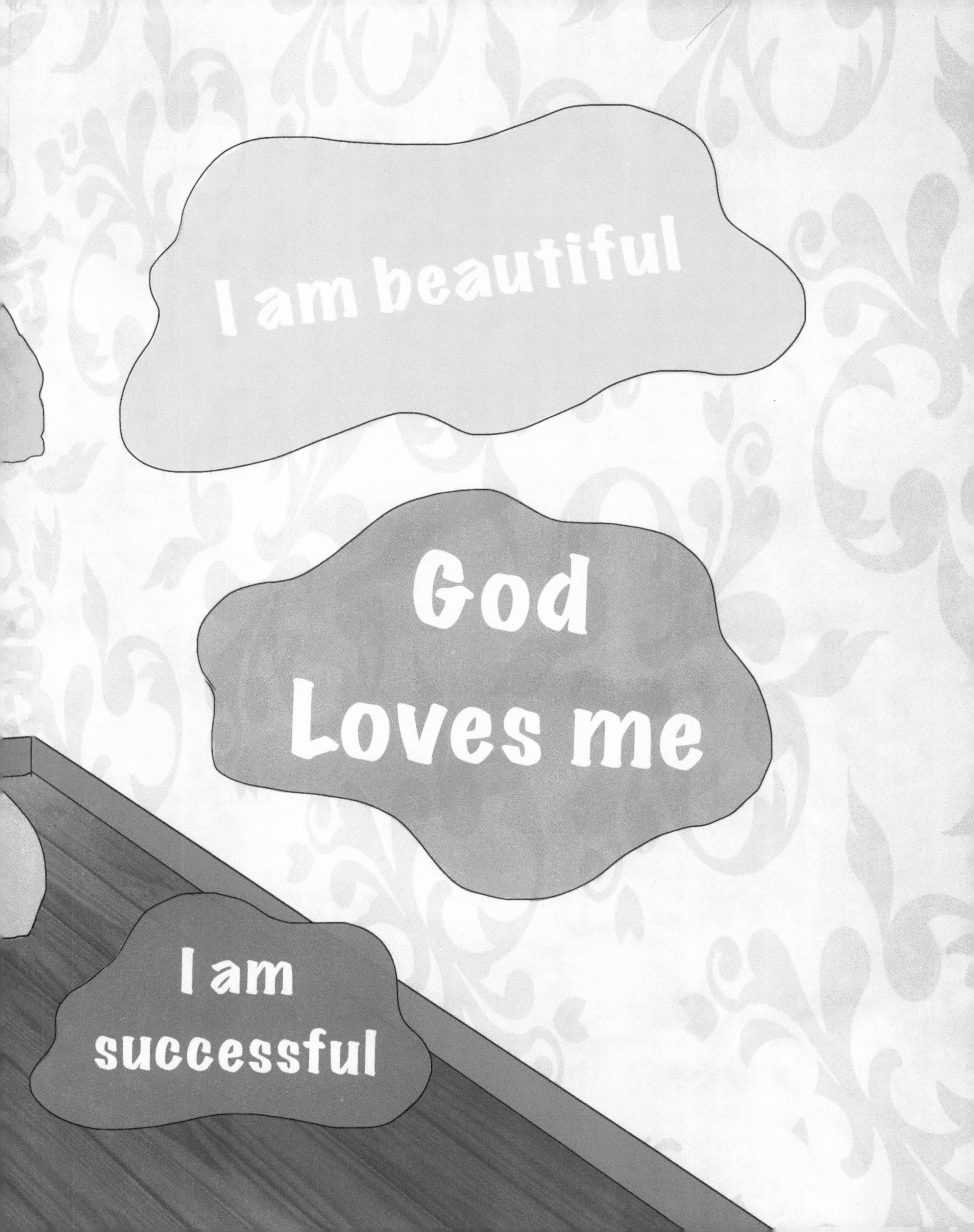
I am beautiful
God Loves me
I am successful

Meet Amayah

Amayah is the daughter of the author and the inspiration for this book. Amayah was born with a Port Wine Stain on her face. Her parents were told by multiple doctors that she should have it removed or cover it up with makeup because it didn't fit society's beauty standards. Heartbroken by these words, her mother decided rather than cover up Amayah's birthmark, she would enourage her to see the beauty in it and love herself just as God made her.

CPSIA information can be obtained
at www.ICGtesting.com
Printed in the USA
BVHW090625011221
622792BV00004B/116